~Bone Deep~

Bone Deep

Deeper than flesh

Deeper than blood

Deeper than family

By Kalen Dion

~Bone Deep~

Copyright 2020 by Kalen M. Dion

All rights reserved. No part of this book may be reproduced or used in any manner, by any means, electronic or mechanical, without express written permission of the copyright owner except for instances of cited quotations and book reviews.

First edition paperback and digital September, 2020

Book design and content by Kalen M. Dion

ISBN: 9798677296512 (Paperback)

This book is the registered property of
Kalen M. Dion/ArtbyKalen

~Bone Deep~

I come out of the closet. I soak the rest of the house in gasoline. I strike a match. I go back into the closet. I gamble with your skeletons and win the souls of your unborn children. The wood speaks the language of crumbling bones. The fire goes quiet.

I am the only survivor.

~Bone Deep~

You know what emotional baggage is?

It's carrying around another persons dirty laundry

so their home doesn't look like a mess.

I'm done wearing other peoples dirt so they don't have to...

and do you know what they call this part of the story?

Coming Clean

~Bone Deep~

I am filing for divorce

with everyone and everything

that doesn't enrich my life.

~Bone Deep~

If I come across as harsh or overly tempered, it is because for the first time in my life, I am learning to advocate for myself. I have allowed people to shit on me and said sorry for creating a stink. I have allowed people to walk on me and apologized for scuffing their shoes.

I have been trying to find an excuse for the fact that I even exist for as long as I can remember.

I am just now learning to speak loud enough to be heard.

Please be patient while I adjust the volume of my emotions.

~Bone Deep~

I spend most of my days

grieving lifetimes

I lost to the fire.

~Bone Deep~

The tears

you never learn to shed as a child

become the fire

you never learn to control as an adult.

~smoke & cloud

~Bone Deep~

Her name is Life.

She is a cruel bitch.

I am filing for divorce.

~ideation

                                   (She's gonna take it all anyway)

~Bone Deep~

I will no longer be calling it cognitive dissonance...

from now on it shall be known as gaslighting for dummies.

~Bone Deep~

If you feed the silence long enough,

it'll grow big enough to swallow your dreams.

~Bone Deep~

Pay attention to the language they use.

You are a survivor...

but abusers...

they will call you a victim.

~just because it came from fire,

                doesn't mean it's smoke

~Bone Deep~

His name is Mirror.

He is a sad and broken man.

I am filing for divorce.

~reflections

(I got sick of bleeding from his wounds)

~Bone Deep~

This is the part of the story

where the love and light go quiet.

This is the part of the story

where you make peace

with the demons

where you dance in the flames

and see what angels are really made of.

~Bone Deep~

I am no longer calling it romantic interest...

from now on it shall be known as chemical roulette.

~Bone Deep~

He is man... he is child.

He was groomed from a young age

to lock away tender and mature.

His focus is conquest;

emotional, physical, sexual.

If it isn't carnal desire

or a method of subjugation,

it is a weakness.

I am filing for divorce.

~Bone Deep~

Her name is Change.

She is scared to death of forever.

I am filing for divorce.

~relentless

(What mask are we wearing today?)

~Bone Deep~

If you aren't serving

101 proof

genuine authentic

I'm not joining you for a drink.

~gasoline, ethanol, and other things that burn easy

~Bone Deep~

The very first thing

abuse does

is it puts on a smile

and talks about undying love.

Abuse asks if you would like water,

then it feeds you to the fire.

~Bone Deep~

If they discourage your pain, your suffering, your grief. If they try to keep your darkness from finding its words. If they ask you to wear a mask made of quiet. It is probably because your sorrow sounds too much like the tears that are falling from the child inside. Too much like the inner voice they are desperately trying to silence. Too much like the skeletons in their closet.

~Bone Deep~

If the word victim

makes you more uncomfortable than the word predator,

you might be standing up for the wrong people.

~burn

~Bone Deep~

His name is Narcissist.

He is the only one in the room.

I am filing for divorce.

~revolve

(It was all about him anyway)

~Bone Deep~

I will no longer be calling them politicians...

from now on they will be known as brokers for the ethically impaired.

~Bone Deep~

I'm not here to knock on doors.

I'm not here to tear down walls.

I'm here

to burn.

the whole.

Fucking.

house.

down.

I see that you're uncomfortable.

It might be time to step outside of your comfort zone.

Shit is about to get hot.

~Bone Deep~

I am not adjusting my boundaries to make room for the thrill you get when you see how your attacks on my sense of self worth bring me discomfort.

~match sticks

~Bone Deep~

My family and I aren't on speaking terms.

I don't know how to hold myself accountable for the things they did to me.

~combustible

~Bone Deep~

Narcissism is not an over inflated sense of self worth. It is a toxic obsession with self promotion, an inability to distinguish lines of autonomy, recognize or respect boundaries, and an unhealthy fixation with self glorification. Narcissism is not an unhealthy love of ones self. It is what happens when one over-compensates for their inability to self love.

~Bone Deep~

Her name is Jealousy.

She owns everything.

I am filing for divorce.

~possession

(She was getting rid of me anyway)

~Bone Deep~

They are two disasters

on a collision course with fate,

dropping love bombs into each others voids,

trying to set the emptiness on fire.

~chemical burns

~Bone Deep~

I will no longer be calling them writers...

from now on they will be known as creators who are nocturnally impaired.

~Bone Deep~

An alcoholic walks into a bar.

He loses his job,

his wife,

his family,

his child,

his dignity,

and his faith.

I was once this man...

Yeah, I know.

I'm still waiting for the punchline too.

~Bone Deep~

~Bone Deep~

The abuser will tell you to accept responsibility for your life. That it is time to move on. They will tell you that you are grown now. They will side track the conversation. They will not say the word abuse until they have no other choice. The last avenue of expression will be them denying the abuse. They will try every other method to disassemble the dialogue first.

The family will side with the abuser. The family will not want to co opt the responsibility. The family will want the dialogue to end. Appeasing the abuser will be easier than appeasing the survivor because appeasing the survivor will mean changing behavioral mechanisms and accepting the responsibility for being complicit in the situation.

Do not let this process exhaust you into silence. You are not the only target. Your voice is the key which unlocks many chains.

~Bone Deep~

Her name is Love.

She is a liar.

I am filing for divorce.

~fairytales

(We never met in person anyway)

~Bone Deep~

Too many of us spend years,

decades,

lifetimes;

digging for hope in the graveyard of love.

~Bone Deep~

I am done carrying your baggage.

It will be waiting for you to join it,

just beyond my boundaries.

~smolder

~Bone Deep~

How much of the weight

you are holding

belongs to somebody else?

~Bone Deep~

I will no longer be calling it toxic masculinity…

from now on it shall be known as poison penis power.

~Bone Deep~

Abuse does not need to be a grand act in order to be destructive. The most insidious abuses are the ones that might go years, decades, lifetimes unnoticed, even by the victim.

If someone repeatedly violates your boundaries, works at creating discomfort, and undercuts your value or sense of self worth, they are abusing you.

Today I build a wall, today I protect my autonomy, today I draw a boundary that they will never cross.

~Bone Deep~

I don't build walls.

I AM a fucking wall.

I dare you to try and climb me.

~skyscraper

~Bone Deep~

They are showing you their colors.

Stop looking away.

~Bone Deep~

Critiques of ones truth, sidelong and judgmental glances at moments of excitement, repeatedly questioning the same facts that have already been clearly stated, ignoring social queues and prying for information or interaction that clearly causes discomfort, disregarding physical and emotional safe spaces and boundaries, using "interrogation" dialogue to keep the target on the defensive and constantly in a responsive cycle, thus controlling the flow of the discussion, sidetracking conversations that promote and encourage ones strength, subtle nods to past conflicts, discrediting accomplishments or changing the subject when personal accomplishments come up, speaking over to extol their own virtues, being distracting to others when one is presenting or speaking, creating a target in every audience, This is how manipulators and narcissists alienate and provoke while looking like the good guy.

Pay attention to the people who use these tactics. Pay attention to who they are targeting. This is how you identify the abuser and the abused.

~Bone Deep~

I am under no obligation

to be silent about my abuses.

Your shame is unconvincing.

If my trauma makes you uncomfortable...

it is time for you to leave.

~scorch

~Bone Deep~

His name is Me.

He doesn't love himself.

I am filing for divorce.

~the longest goodbye

(I know that I deserve better)

~Bone Deep~

He seemed like such a nice guy is the sound of domestic violence, molestation, murder, rape.

He seemed like such a nice guy is what blind eyes say when they are forced open.

~forensics

~Bone Deep~

Her name is Tomorrow.

She is made mostly of unreasonable expectations.

I am filing for divorce.

~out of touch

(I was never going to be enough anyway)

~Bone Deep~

Your shit behavior is the problem.

Not the fact that I called it out.

Now get the fuck out of here with your gas-lighty bull shit.

~residue

~Bone Deep~

They will slap a ribbon and a gift tag on neglect. They will wrap it in a box labeled love. They will place it under your Christmas tree and ask you why you aren't more grateful.

~Bone Deep~

His name is yesterday.

He won't let me grow.

I am filing for divorce.

~wilt

(Some of them don't want you to bloom)

~Bone Deep~

Ashes

~Bone Deep~

~Bone Deep~

About the Author

Kalen Dion is an Author and artist working out of Southern California. Extroverted and dynamic, with a keen regard for the spiritual aspects of the human experience, his work highlights the struggles of recovery, alcoholism, abuse, and trauma, by focusing on the development of coping mechanisms, self care techniques, as well as a deep love and respect for all walks of life.

Made in the USA
Middletown, DE
26 January 2022